HERE IS WATER

'GBENGA ADEOBA

Published by Akashic Books
©2019 'Gbenga Adeoba

ISBN: 978-1-61775-739-6

Printed in China
First printing

Akashic Books
Brooklyn, New York, USA
Ballydehob, Co. Cork, Ireland
Twitter: @AkashicBooks
Facebook: AkashicBooks
E-mail: info@akashicbooks.com
Website: www.akashicbooks.com

African Poetry Book Fund
Prairie Schooner
University of Nebraska
110 Andrews Hall
Lincoln, Nebraska 68588

TABLE OF CONTENTS

PREFACE
by Sholeh Wolpé

I read 'Gbenga Adeoba's *Here is Water* while traveling high above the Pacific. The plane dips then shudders. The woman next to me grasps her seat handle and shrieks. She makes an airy noise fraught with anxiety. Soon enough the seatbelt light flickers off, and we are back to smooth sailing in our seats equipped with music and movies, blankets and pillows. My comfort and security contrasts the poignancy and heartbreak I feel reading Adeoba's poems—his "parables of no return" on the waters of the Mediterranean where the sea shifts, "heralding / its cargo in quick syllables of an onrush."

> Bordered by kelps—brown murals supple as wool—
> and a cloud of winged witnesses,
> our boat is somewhere in the middle of the Mediterranean,
> miles and miles from the coast near Tobruk
> in Libya, where we had camped until the smugglers
> and the sea spoke of its fidelity.

The drama of terror and sadness that unfolds in these poems, physically and symbolically, is around Lampedusa, the European territory closest to Libya which—since the beginning of the century—has become a prime transit point for migrants from Africa.

> What binds us now is a known fear,
> a kinship of likely loss, the understanding that we, too,
> could become a band of unnamed migrants
> found floating on the face of the sea.

In 2015 alone, within the space of four months, close to 1,600 migrants died braving the sea towards this small Sicilian province, making it one of the deadliest migrant routes in the world. A horrifying human tragedy in a world of growing displacement and injustice.

I put my palm to my mouth and read each poem under my breath. They read like hymns of hopes and dreams rhythmed with refrains of loss—a horrifying concert on the sea. In this instance, an unfaithful sea. A sea that holds the promise of passage to a better life but instead devours the hopeful like a hungry beast. Hence the vehicle becomes the destination.

In poem after poem Adeoba plunges us with merciless literary grace into a world where waves become shrouds that wrap themselves around "fragments of lived lives." Men, women, and children become "a band of unnamed migrants / found floating on the face of the sea." This generic bundling of human beings into "migrants"—deliberately viewed from a distant narrator's Western perspective—is intentional. By doing so, Adeoba draws attention to the need for the specificities of memory. He fluidly transports us between the beginnings and ends of dreams, replete with lives in water. Here are women who huddle in "little boats" like "modern slaves," holding tight to their songs and wisdom in dialects of their land; women who left their families because they themselves had already begun to drown; mothers and daughters who left oppressive homes to survive. The weight of these women's grief cannot keep them afloat on a ravenous sea.

> They huddle even in death;
> their mouths shaped as though
> they wanted to say what we do not know,
> how far they had gone that November morning,
> in the sure calm of dawn, before the sea,
> ageless, raised the cost of passage.

Here is Water is cinematic music; it moves with liquid ease between dreams and drowning, faith and unfaithfulness, hope and hollowness. Tokens from the past open pathways into imagination:

> An old photograph,
> sewn into the inner pocket
> of his caftan, offers you a reel
> from the dream he sewed to the sea.

When Adeoba writes of the "pull of tides" to "[reinvent] the shore / into a space of things intimate and lost," you intuitively brace yourself for what is coming, almost afraid to read on. Refrains of "loss is upon us" repeat like waves in a sea that holds "the lexicon of memory." This sea of tears carries so much loss it changes "the texture" of eyes. This is not a comfortable sea where we go to gaze or meditate. Adeoba's sea is a restless cold grave that spits onto its shores "trinket boxes," a "girl's / plastic doll," or "[a baby's] shoes."

Although *Here is Water* is a book about loss and longing, it is also solidly about memory that Adeoba refuses to let settle into a "coat of rust." Instead, he leads our eyes "into days / wide and free like open waters" and tenderly weaves lives together into meaning:

> These pictures
> are how I sedate longing into stillness.
> Sometimes a tug or the craft of winds;
> another time, desire glides,
> courses through me like the ease
> of water receding, nursing its intentions.

I press my forehead to the plane window and try to make out the contours of the sea below, its waves crisscrossing in a foamy alphabet of Adeoba's dead. I have un-learned what I thought I knew about the sea and "the posture of water."

A FUNERAL HYMN IN FALSETTO

February 1, 2006

On the night my grandfather rejected tea
and offered his last breath instead,
the earth shifted an inch.
And I listened out for a rustle of leaves
or a flash of thunder
amidst the wailers' phonation.

At the funeral,
when the chorister sang
the paradise hymn in falsetto,
I imagined a brood of angels
heralding the arrival of my grandfather
who was migrating in a boat of glass.

It is a decade now,
and sighs have replaced hymns
in the order of memories.
The elegies, too, return to me
the way an empty alley
returns our gift of words in multiples.

SEAFARERS

> *The sea is History.*
> —Derek Walcott

The refrain of this water says something
is imminent, says loss is upon us.

Bordered by kelps—brown murals supple as wool—
and a cloud of winged witnesses,
our boat is somewhere in the middle of the Mediterranean,
miles and miles from the coast near Tobruk
in Libya, where we had camped until the smugglers
and the sea spoke of its fidelity.

It was a soft, fluid tune:
the tender draw of water, a rare liquid craft—
the sea, keen, humming a promise of calm,
urging us to draw closer, to unlearn
all we thought we knew about the posture of water.

There are dismembered boat parts, whole dinghies, too,
shooting out from somewhere beneath this expanse, yielding us
to catalogues of told and untold mishaps,
the sea's unfulfilled promises to those who had knocked
on its door, those who sought to know its ways:

the Nigerian boy, wan as wilted fruit, comforting his sister,
after they lost their mother miles away from Sabratha,
and those with whom we had camped at the coast,
the ones who drowned overnight

some hundred miles south of the Island of Lampedusa.

What binds us now is a known fear,
a kinship of likely loss, the understanding that we, too,
could become a band of unnamed migrants
found floating on the face of the sea

or swept ashore by wave upon wave
on a beach west of Tripoli.

RESURRECTION

along the coasts of Northern Africa

On the fortnight of your return,
they would bunch around the evening fire
to learn of your resurrection: the unhallowed season
of the sea, the throes, the convention of birds
on the route where the smugglers
joined you to a truck towards the waters;
and the sovereignty of dust in half-empty towns,
past the caves and their autonomy of green—
foliages retelling parables of no return.
How the sea beyond keeps no record
of the drowned and those it washed ashore,
how you, too, are a Lazarus of the Nile.

NIGHTSHIFT AT THE COAST

*When we are gone
our lives will continue without us.*
                              —John Burnside

This light, the burst
 and softness of its insistence,

bidding you to be still is holding
the expanse in a meld of brown and red.

From the coast,
you can see the weight
of its sheen pressed on cowries
swept ashore, cuddling in seawater.

It is the same trick artificial lights
play on water, daring an undoing.

There is an intimation of memory
in its stance,

this being your fortyish season
of translating the cryptography
of such early lights into lexicons
known to the eyes.

There are no limits
now to the sway of the glow;

considering the leaves,
blown seawards, yielding,
unfurling their inner lives.
The sea, too, urging a reintroduction,
becoming what you do not know.

When you check the stretch again,
you find him face-first in the shroud of a wave.

The sea, shifting, heralding
its cargo in quick syllables of an onrush.

The gash and grime on his body
witnessing to the long sail from the waters,
off the coast of Sabratha,
where the smugglers' dinghies mostly drown.

An old photograph,
sewn into the inner pocket
of his caftan, offers you a reel
from the dream he sowed to the sea:

he, barefooted on a football field,
donning the jersey of an Italian team;

the half-smile on his face,
like a butterfly with one wing,

almost beautiful.

LEAVING AGADEZ

They all cling to remains
of safety in this truck careening
towards Sabha in Libya.

They crowd the back,
shrouded in a half-light
haloing their bodies—

the broken windows
opening into Asmara, Raqqa,
Darfur, and other cathedrals of war.

When they collate their aches,
it is in whispers—

a longing to break this ruse,

the pact between the smugglers
and songbirds governing
this region,

the insistence of gusts sweeping
the desert, building Babel again.

Too frail to bear the angst,
the kids on board are crying.

They are asking their parents
if they will make it,

if they all won't be sold again
before they get to Sabha, or Tripoli,
where they can make for the waters.

Knowing the chances are a binary,
the adults are hesitant.

They know they could be sold again,

they could get caught
by the guards who would shout
emshi, emshi*,
deporting them back to Agadez,

to those camps where comrades
who have failed in this quest reside,

often staying awake in full moons,
mourning dreams forgone.

Emshi means leave in Arabic

CHILD OF THE WORLD

after Ibukun Adeeko's "Visiting Waters,"
Kechi Nomu's "Old Bones Seeking Wooden Crosses"

You want to walk on water so bad
or tell your father you know
what it is to sin,
but you let him pile dreams broken on you instead.
　　　　—Kechi Nomu

Because his father said water,
not words, was the beginning
of all things, the boy sits often
by the river where he was named.
The aloes, ferns, and bulrushes
are, to him, a wall of kindness.
He would bend his ears
to the ensemble of ripples;
or, when the fishermen were
all gone, he would ford the waters
in search of depths where he
could drown his weight of years.
His father said: Son, what you seek
to drown is not a name; it is history.
His father said he was named
for the rust of songs, scars of Libya,
and the gray vaults of the sea.
He said he was named
for drowned men the world over,
his watered flax and tulips
that didn't blossom,
the dream of years withering still.

HALF-ACRE OF WATER

A mass funeral was held on Friday in Salerno, Italy for 26 young Nige-
rian women who drowned while trying to cross the Mediterranean Sea.
                    —*Sahara Reporters,* November 17, 2017

Gulls, too, are fleeing that portion
where their bodies were drowned,
those Nigerian women, 26 of them.

They had begun to drown those many years
ago—in homes that were no longer homes—
long before they made for the waters,
keen as early birds, under the dark witness
of nights; when they said only the sea
could bear the weight of their grief.

They huddle even in death;
their mouths shaped as though
they wanted to say what we do not know,
how far they had gone that November morning,
in the sure calm of dawn, before the sea,
ageless, raised the cost of passage.

But there are no words now,
only the fragments of lived lives
flung about in that half-acre of water;

the birds pitching their grief from a distance,
mourning the loss—these women that
would rest in the Italy they never knew.

THE MORNING AFTER

at an IDP camp in Borno, Northern Nigeria

Only water could bond them stronger
than the kinship of loss, these little ones in Rann,
far north of Borno, singing and jumping in the rain—
a respite for the dust and their parched hearts.
Their ears quick to thunderclaps, weaker than
the booms that claimed their kindred five months earlier.
The tiny lights in their eyes twinkling a longing.
Despite that downpour, the sing-song
of school tunes, the ones they learnt from UNICEF
workers, fill the spaces hidden from the rain, from fire.
The morning after, a girl would sit, half-awake,
drifted twigs and leaves around her like mourners,
under the dogoyaro tree where they had fraternized,
singing the unbroken beatitudes of rain,
lending their voices to the rhythm of water;
the light in her eyes weak like the effort of dawn,
her tiny fingers mapping her arms,
the henna drawings darker now, feeling for an opening,
for the tender touches she lost to the fire.

HERE IS WATER

after Kechi Nomu's Old Bones Seeking Wooden Crosses

At the waterside in Boyo, the
rituals of movement intensify at dusk.

The pull of tides reinvents the shore
into a space for things intimate and lost.

You could find trinket boxes or a girl's
plastic doll in that rubble. Baby shoes, too.

The tiny things are heavier—even songbirds.
I am thinking these tunes being telegraphed

into the dark, fretting the waters,
are a tribute to the lives of drowned men.

I sit by the water, knowing how
sounds could alter the shape of an expanse.

The boys who walk the boundaries now,
in search of collectibles, bear on their bodies

a history threaded to this river.
One wades inward: water around his body;

water, a different texture, in his eyes.
He pulls two of his friends along,

past the quay where the barges
and their fathers' canoes used to lay.

Here is water, he says.
Here is memory shifting in its form,

bearing things heavy and lost. My father
and yours, here now and gone like the tides.

WHAT BIRDS SING OF IN LIBYA

after Ross Kemp

In Brak, Surman, and places in Libya governed
by water, what breaks the night is mostly songs—

the lilt, the open pulse of thrushes warbling
their cadence, casting their burdens upon the waters;
the sheer miracle of Aves urging men to love again,
calling them to images craving tenderness:

Migrants, modern slaves, huddled on little boats,
crossing the Mediterranean—a grave wide enough
for the numbers—into the unknown, through the same routes
desert septs took while importing human commodities
into North Africa three centuries ago.

On tonight's playlist, there are moving birdsongs
for wishes that survive the desert but end in dinghies
ferrying the favoured bunches to unnamed countries,
to likely death; some more for women,
hopeful housemaids, who have their Italy-bound dreams
diverted to desert brothels; or young men in captive,
crying, praying their ransom.

The flock, unwavering, dissecting the waters
with their rhythm, preaching love yet again,
calling humanity to the loss of itself.

ECLIPSE

at a slave port in Dahomey, old Benin Republic

All night, they had waited for the Captain's blast—
an initiation into a ritual, piercing as a dark prophecy—
so that the ship would sail away from the piers
into a future unfolding in fetters.
There seemed to be an urgency on the sea,
a rhythm of narrowness,
and it was unlike the tune they had learned:
to be wide and free like this water.
Ripples, too, the sheer liturgy of liquid bodies.
Held within the crevices of each ripple
were tossed dreams, rehearsed scenes
and unheard songs, the lexicon of memory
and wisdom told in Bariba, Fon and Fula*,
unwinding, reeling into that Dahomeyan pallor
and the soft pockets of the sea.
And for once, they knew their dreams, too,
would ebb into a patina speaking only in whispers,
the language of a body speaking to itself.

Bariba, Fon and Fula are dialects in Benin Republic

MIDDLE PASSAGE

an unreported shipwreck, circa 1761

"Sirs, I perceive that the voyage will be with injury
and much loss, not only of the cargo and the ship,
but also of our lives." Acts 27:10

It was nothing like a trainee sailor's imagination
of the sea or the infirmity of rudders.
But it got darker there in that lacklustre region
where the vessel, coasting, tuned out of Zanzibar,
where the sail seemed to have given in
to the wind's insistence on a wreck. It would take a slave
or two to pacify this water psalming a ruin.
Maybe it took more: we would later hear of David,
not Livingstone, who lost his fortune (or his fortune lost him).
Dawson, too, darling of Kings and warlords;
his accordion, chest, and rum dreams.
No daily had enough room for this loss, those slaves
huddled in the ship cell as a cluster, singing,
knitting their sing-song into the thick of that hurricane.

PA CUDJO LEWIS WEAVES A SONG

after Peter Akinlabi

A night so weak it leans on
a cane of light, a lunar index of
grief, he sits still in Alabama's dark,
adrift of the sea of his life, the waves
of loss—five sons and a daughter gone
in their prime, lying still in Old Plateau.

Age has pulled a mask on
the face he could call his, the one
his woman, Abile, didn't know.

A Baptist hymn, elegiac,
pedals through Africatown.
He reimagines Bante, that far home,
now: the unfurling of songs and riddles
told on ledges, the tongues of fire;

or women, in a loop of grief,
mourning husbands and lost sons,
mornings after they were captured
and herded through tunnels of green,

through Abomey and Ouidah,
to a two-masted schooner perched
on the waters like a bird in rest. The
boys singing their ache to the wind.

The hymn, louder now, wafts

into his invented space, urging a
shift from the posture of memory.

He weaves this burden
of remembrance into a different
form, lore told to the twin girls—
Mary and Martha—looking into
his eyes as unto a prophecy; his voice
quaking as he spoke—one song for
every little light going out in his heart.

HERMIT

The day your body is finally found
in the near-empty room with fluttering blinds,
all that will be left is a web of memories:
a detained cadaver awaiting medics' trial;
the relics of your library,
a finger-marked pick that reveals
"A Thousand Ways to Die (For Dummies)."

Your abridged biography, a forlorn,
picture-starved obituary, will appear in
the next day's dailies or the next.
Unlike a death note,
it will not tell the world why you left,
how you dined with death in piecemeal.
How, like David, you read Psalm 51
after every rehearsal of your suicide.

OPEN WATERS

Here, I am owning the moments
again—each contour of light, every
slice of grace pressed into the shutter.
I make meaning of them. These pictures
are how I sedate longing into stillness.
Sometimes a tug or the craft of winds;
another time, desire glides,
courses through me like the ease
of water receding, nursing its intentions.
The years behind arc into years,
but things here do not wear their
coat of rust. They furl hems around
petals, your eyes leading into days
wide and free like open waters.

ACKNOWLEDGMENTS

The following poems have appeared in these publications:

"Seafarers," *Poet Lore*
"Resurrection" and "What birds sing of in Libya," *Prairie Schooner*
"Eclipse," *Pleiades*
"Middle Passage," *Notre Dame Review*
"A funeral hymn in falsetto," *Salamander*
"Hermit," *Phases: Poetry of People* (Anthology)